5 Minute Devotions
for the
HOMESCHOOL
MOM

TINA NAHID

CONTENTS

Preface

About the Author

Preface

My desire in writing this devotional is to give all of you amazing homeschool moms a moment of rest and some food for thought on this often bone-weary, but joyful, journey called homeschooling.

I pray that you find a breath of fresh air and that you can relax and enjoy a quiet moment, heart to heart, with another mom who understands the real ups and downs, all too well.

May the Lord bless you as you take five minutes to breath and enjoy.

Tina

Who's In Control

A codependent person is one who has let another person's behavior affect him or her and who is obsessed with controlling that person's behavior.
—Melody Beattie

The issue of control.

Yes, it's an issue that many homeschool moms wrestle with daily. And most of us don't even realize it. How do we guide, teach, and help our children, without crossing the line into codependency and control? How do we keep a healthy balance in our relationships with our children?

Using the word "codependent" to describe this type of behavior may be new, or even shocking, to some of us. We have often heard this term used as a definition for those who have been married to an addict; someone who has been an enabler or victim. Yet, this term carries a much broader scope. It includes a desire to control someone else's behavior to the detriment of all those involved.

I have certainly been guilty of this myself with my own children. I have felt that all of their choices, behaviors, attitudes, etc., are directly affecting me and my life; that somehow all of their choices are a direct reflection of me. So in order to feel better about me, I feel as though I must control their choices, their decisions, and their lives!

Not only is this exhausting physically, but emotionally, mentally and spiritually draining as well. It's time to begin to break free. Knowledge and understanding of our struggles begins the process of freedom. Letting Jesus have ALL the control and seeking Him for wisdom is the starting point. We must acknowledge that we are powerless over our tendency to be controlling and allow His Spirit and power to flow through us each and every moment; this is a key to joy in our homeschooling journey.

Scripture for Meditation:
Humble yourselves, therefore, under God's mighty hand, that he may lift you up in due time. Cast all your anxiety on him because he cares for you.
–1 Peter 5:6-7

Prayer for Today:
Father, I humbly come before You and cast all my cares upon You, today. I ask You for wisdom on how to live an emotionally healthy life with my children and spouse, walking along side of them. Set me free from the compulsion to control others around me, and heal me of all the wounds that have caused any codependent behavior. Thank you, Jesus. Amen.

Vital Boundaries

The truth is, we tend to train people how we want to be treated. If others know you have wishy-washy boundaries then they are free to walk all over you; the results...you become a doormat. We have actually trained others to do this when we will allow people to wipe their muddy feet on us. After all, we are doormats.
—David W. Earle

Boundaries. What a loaded word! In my own personal experience, and in those of other homeschooling moms, I know there seems to be a real struggle with the concept of boundaries. After all, we are "in charge" of our children's physical, emotional, spiritual, academic and mental welfare the majority of each day. Whew. It can be a heavy load to carry!

Yet, if we desire to walk in health and peace as moms, we must learn the vital importance of having boundaries in our lives. We cannot say yes to every good opportunity for our children. We cannot sign up for every ministry opportunity that comes our way. We cannot clean and pick up continually after our children without requiring them to share in the responsibilities at home. We cannot put off taking care of our physical bodies in order to make the needs of others more important.

This may not sound very "Christian" to you. This is because many of us believe the lies that twist scriptures into saying things that they have never said! God is a God of boundaries. Jesus had boundaries. Boundaries are crucial for all people. They protect us and help us to be the best we can be for the Lord and for those we love. If we don't teach our children boundaries by our example, how will they learn? Do we want them to become controllers and dictators of others or, on the flip side, someone's doormat?

Today, you have permission to use a wonderful little word…NO. Say it over and over again. Get used to the way it feels. Empowering, isn't it? It's awkward at first, but as you learn to say it, it's freeing. We cannot do it all, nor were we made to. We must walk in the calling and the guidance that we have, and that's enough. We can walk in peace and freedom and with boundaries firmly in place.

Scripture for Meditation:
We will not boast about things done outside our area of authority. We will boast only about what has happened within the **boundaries** of the work God has given us, which includes our working with you.
–2 Corinthians 10:13

Prayer for Today:
Father, thank You for healthy boundaries that You have created for our lives. We pray for wisdom to implement these boundaries in our lives in a balanced and loving way. Help us to teach our children, by our example, what boundaries look like and why they are important for us. Thank you, Lord. Amen.

The Power of Play

When we treat children's play as seriously as it deserves, we are helping them feel the joy that's to be found in the creative spirit. It's the things we play with and the people who help us play that make a great difference in our lives.
—Fred Rogers

Play.
Playing with my children…

I will admit this is an area that I must be more pro-active and diligent about. It seems when my children were younger, it was a little easier to play with them, to put everything else aside and just focus on play. Yet, the longer we go in our homeschooling journey, the easier it is to focus on the "to-do" list rather than the "play list."

Yet, I think as parents, we lose a great deal of life's simple enjoyments if we don't stop our agendas and take time simply to "be" with our children, no matter what their age. Personally, I have never been very enthused about playing tea party or imaginary games with my kids. It's just more torture to me than anything else! And that's okay. As parents, we must accept that there are some things that we just can't do. Yet, what are the things that we can enjoy playing with our children? A good game of Scrabble? A card game? Reading books aloud to our children? Going outside and throwing or kicking a ball?

These are all wonderful forms of play for our children. And they love for us to be engaged with them. Sometimes,

I fall into the mentality that since I am physically present with my children all day, through homeschooling, that somehow that negates the importance of me actually *engaging* with them in something they simply enjoy. I often let housework or other duties take priority over play. It's a struggle, but I do believe it's a worthwhile pursuit.

One tip I have found to be helpful, in this regard, is to set a timer and tell my children that I can play with them for a certain amount of time, but when the timer goes off, I have to move on to something else. This gives me a better sense of "start and stop" time and helps me to focus while I am engaging in their particular activity. I believe whatever we can do to incorporate more fun and bonding into our day is well worth it!

Scripture for Meditation:
One day some parents brought their children to Jesus so he could lay his hands on them and pray for them. But the disciples scolded the parents for bothering him. But Jesus said, "Let the children co me to me. Don't stop them! For the Kingdom of Heaven belongs to those who are like these children." And he placed his hands on their heads and blessed them before he left.
–Matthew 19:13-15

Prayer for Today:
Father, I pray for the grace to "stop and play"…to play with my children, to enjoy simply being with them. Help us to find common areas of enjoyment and pleasure so that I can bond with each of them and make memories that will last a lifetime. Help me to overcome the need to perform and accomplish my "to-do" list and to rest in Your love and peace. Amen.

The Highest Education

The giving of love is an education in itself.
—Eleanor Roosevelt

It seems that, often, as homeschool moms, we give and give and give…and give some more! We are always giving to our children; giving them structure for their days, giving them books and curriculum which we have researched and chosen for them, giving them our time in helping them with their lessons, giving them food, shelter, toys…and on and on it goes.

But sometimes, in the midst of all this giving, it's easy to forget the most important thing we have to give…our love and acceptance. This may be in the form of an encouraging word, a gentle hug, and a smile. In all of our rush to make our homeschools "the best", we forget the most important and singular aspect of our days upon this earth.

What will our children remember about their life at home with us? Will they remember feeling pressured and tense? Will they remember how they felt they had to "perform" in order to secure our love? Or will they remember what a warm and inviting place their home was and how safe and secure they felt being there?

Giving them these memories to store up in the banks is, by far, the most important aspect of our homeschooling days with them. I am learning this myself. I am a work in progress. I have failed…miserably at times. If you feel this way, you are not alone. Take heart. It's not too late to refocus and change our directions and goals. Our Father's grace is available abundantly to all who seek Him.

Scripture for Meditation:
If I could speak all the languages of earth and of angels, but didn't love others, I would only be a noisy gong or a clanging cymbal. If I had the gift of prophecy, and if I understood all of God's secret plans and possessed all knowledge, and if I had such faith that I could move mountains, but didn't love others, I would be nothing. If I gave everything I have to the poor and even sacrificed my body, I could boast about it; but if I didn't love others, I would have gained nothing.
–1 Corinthians 13:1-3

Prayer for Today: *Abba Father, I come to ask You to fill me with Your love for my children. Reorient my goals to be focused on giving my children an education of love, above and beyond anything else that I may give them. Help me to shift my goals toward this highest pursuit. And help me to experience your Divine Love for me daily, so that I can, in turn, let this love flow through me onto those around me. Amen.*

The Divine Spark

If you have anything really valuable to contribute to the world it will come through the expression of your own personality, that single spark of divinity that sets you off and makes you different from every other living creature.
—Bruce Barton

The divine spark.

Every human being has been created in the image of our Creator God. Thus, we all carry a unique "spark" of the Divine within us. How amazing is this? How awesome! But, oh, how often we miss this truth in our daily lives, in the lives of not only our children but ourselves as well. Sometimes we are so bogged down and conformed to the world around us that we become only a shadow of who we were really meant to be.

Educating our children at home offers a unique opportunity for us, as moms, to capture the "divine sparks" of our children and harness their potential in countless ways. Yet, sadly, in my case, I find that my need to "control" their behavior often snuffs out the creative "sparks" that make them who they are. I am becoming more and more aware of this controlling tendency, and I am thankful the Holy Spirit is illuminating this issue in my life.

Our children are not cookie-cutter people. We don't really want them to be, do we? Not deep down. We want them to flourish and thrive as the unique and special individuals they were created to be. Yet, forcing them into a "box", when it comes to their learning, will not achieve this end. Allowing them more freedom to direct their own learning and giving them options and choices in exploring the world around them will prove far more beneficial to them as they mature.

Let's allow this paradigm shift to begin to sink in today. Let's not only allow their differences to manifest, but let's celebrate those distinct differences in our children, and in ourselves as well! Let's think about how their education could be tailored specifically to their own personalities and gifts. There are a variety of ways in which we can do this. Let's just follow the Holy Spirit's lead.

Scripture for Meditation:
You made all the delicate, inner parts of my body and knit me together in my mother's womb. Thank you for making me so wonderfully complex! Your workmanship is marvelous—how well I know it.
–Psalm 139:13-14

Prayer for Today: *Dearest Abba, thank You for creating me with a spark of who You are. Thank You for your amazing love to create human beings in your image. Help me to become more aware of my children's unique personalities, and help me to give them more freedom and self-direction in their education, and to trust You instead of trying to be controlling. Amen.*

Self Care Isn't Selfish...
It's Essential

Growing into your future with health and grace and beauty doesn't have to take all your time. It rather requires a dedication to caring for yourself as if you were rare and precious, which you are, and regarding all life around you as equally so, which it is.
—Victoria Moran

As a stay-at-home and homeschooling mom, I have often fallen into the martyr syndrome. You may also be afflicted with this syndrome; which basically feeds us the lie that we don't have time to take care of ourselves and that our first priority is to take care of others. Even within the church, we somehow are often deceived that in order to truly be a godly woman, we must deny our own needs, even the healthy ones, in order to truly be a servant to others.

I know this lie well. There were many years early in my homeschool years where I felt overwhelmed with what I was doing for my family. I felt as if I was a selfish person for desiring "me-time" or time to pursue something else that I enjoyed. Even exercising at the gym would induce guilt because I was putting my children in the gym's day-care for an hour or two. Somehow I felt that I was being selfish by doing this. Nothing could have been further from the truth!

The truth is, when you take care of your physical, emotional, mental and spiritual needs, then you are putting forth the best you that your family needs! Taking care of our earthly bodies makes us a good steward of what our

Lord has blessed us with. There was a period of a few years where I even neglected to go to the dentist or to get a yearly woman's check-up. I was too busy, or so I thought. I couldn't even take the time to make an appointment. This wasn't wise on my part, and I am very grateful that my health didn't deteriorate beyond repair, during those years.

My message today, dear sister, is that we must take care of ourselves. Going for walks or the gym, going to sit at a coffee or tea shop and read a book, taking time to date our husbands, going out for a mom's night with friends…these are all wonderful pursuits that help to make us better mothers and wives to our children. Let us not believe the lies that we must put all of our own needs aside in order to fulfill our God-given callings to our home and family. Let us embrace the joy that comes for a healthy lifestyle to the glory of God.

Scripture for Meditation:
Do you not know that your bodies are temples of the Holy Spirit, who lives in you and was given to you by God? You do not belong to yourself for God bought you with a high price. So you must honor God with your body.
–1 Corinthians 6:19-20

Prayer for Today: *Dear Father, we are fearfully and wonderfully made. Help us to embrace the joy that comes from taking care of our own needs, and give us the grace to trust You with our lives and bodies. May we walk in the truth and balance in this area of our lives. Amen.*

Relationships over Academics

I once heard a quote that said something to this effect:

"Rules without Relationship lead to Rebellion"

This is so true. It goes along with something the Spirit has been whispering into my heart. He has been encouraging me to ***"focus on the relationships with my children more than their academics."*** This doesn't necessarily come easily or naturally to me, especially with all the added pressure I sometimes carry as a homeschooling parent. Yet, I know, beyond a doubt, that what the Lord is telling me is far more important than my worries about math, history, or any other academic subject!

This is our encouragement for today. Let's focus on our relationships; our heart connections with our children. The rest will come, and the academics will better flow when our hearts our bonded, and our children feel a sense of safety and trust with us as their parents.

Scripture for Meditation:
I, therefore, the prisoner of the Lord, beseech you to walk worthy of the calling with which you were called, with all lowliness and gentleness, with longsuffering, bearing with one another n love, endeavoring to keep the unity of the Spirit in the bond of peace.
–Ephesians 4:1-3

Prayer for Today: *Father, forgive us when we have put more emphasis on academic learning than we have on our relationships and heart connections with our children. Help us to love as You love us, in the way we interact with them on a daily basis. Amen.*

Letting Go of Fear

Knowledge which is acquired under compulsion has no hold on the mind. Therefore do not use compulsion, but let early education be a sort of amusement; you will then be better able to discover the child's natural bent.
—Plato

Wow. It sounds so good! But in reality, it's so hard for many of us as homeschool moms to put into practice. We are so worried that our children may not know certain facts by certain ages that we end up pushing our children and stressing them out, leading them to despise learning in the process.

This is the opposite of what we are trying to achieve with our precious little ones. Our intentions are mostly good. Yet, often we are acting and reacting out of fear; fear of what others think of us, fear of being a failure. We feel this internal pressure to "prove" to the world at large that our children are "okay." And not just "okay," but even that they are "exceptional."

But what are we trying to "prove" exactly? As believers in Christ, we must have an internal desire that points us to an audience of One. Our Father is the only One we should be concerned with when it comes to how we educate our children. And our goal becomes aligned with His...to allow our children to flourish in the gifts, talents, and "ways" they were created...in their own timing.

I truly wish I had put this concept into practice when my oldest son was just a little guy. Instead, I did all the things listed above. I was living out of a fear-based motivation. Oh, if I had it to do over again, how much more I would have enjoyed his childhood years, letting him explore and dream, and putting no "compulsions" on him to do formal bookwork. Learn from my mistakes, and take it from Plato—you will enjoy the journey far more!

Scripture for Meditation:
Direct your children onto the right path, and when they are older, they will not leave it.
–Proverbs 22:6

Prayer for Today:
Father, help me to learn to trust You in the education of my children. Show me their particular bents—their talents, their gifting, their callings. Help me to encourage them in the direction in which You made them, and not my own. I pray You will deliver me from a spirit of fear and help me to surrender all control to You. Amen.

Learning Together

The aim of education should be to teach us rather how to think, than what to think—rather to improve our minds, so as to enable us to think for ourselves, than to load the memory with the thoughts of other men.
—James Beattie

Home schooling is a journey of learning, not only for the child, but also for the parents. We often go into this experience with the mentality that we are going to "teach" our children, rather than to "learn together" with them. As we go along, we realize that we, as the home school parent, need to go through a period of "de-schooling" ourselves.

We often find ourselves "spoon-feeding" our children what and/or how they should think instead of exploring ideas with them and asking probing questions. God's Word is full of great and mysterious truths to explore. All questions should be welcome and not having all the answers is okay! It's a spiritual journey we are on. Even as the parents, we have not arrived!

Discovering "how to think" is generally a very overlooked skill in today's society. It seems everyone is so "conformed" to the societal norms. And even as homeschoolers, who are considered somewhat on the "fringe", we can fall into this conformity mentality. Yet, it helps if we view our home education as a journey of learning and living and loving together, rather than as a set of standards, lists, and rules to follow. Living and walking by faith takes courage and ingenuity. And of these traits, we want our children and ourselves to have an abundance!

Scripture for Meditation:
Don't copy the behavior and customs of this world, but let God transform you into a new person by changing the way you think. Then you will learn to know God's will for you, which is good and pleasing and perfect.
–Romans 12:2

Prayer for Today:
Dear Lord, help us today to learn "with" our children. Teach us "how" to think for ourselves, and not simply what information we need. I pray for Your grace to guide me with wisdom and love on this journey with my family. Amen.

Knowledge of the Ancient Path

Once upon a time, all children were homeschooled. They were not sent away from home each day to a place just for children but lived, learned, worked, and played in the real world, alongside adults and other children of all ages.
—Rachel Gathercole

Isn't this comforting truth? Isn't it wonderful to know that the choices we have made as homeschool moms, in our modern times, are the same choices that have been made by families for thousands of years? Our modern school system is the recent invention of educating children. Yet, it often doesn't seem that way, does it? It's so easy to fall into thinking we are the "outcasts" who have chosen some strange, new path in keeping our children at home with us.

It's important for us as moms to gain as much knowledge as we can about the history and background of home education. The more knowledge and understanding we have concerning the history behind what we are doing, the more we will be able to stand up to the pressures that our put on us in our modern times. The knowledge that we are truly following an "ancient path" is very empowering and can help us persevere, when we would rather give up. And those times do come for most of us! It's a normal part of the process.

Having our children with us is possibly more difficult for us, as modern women, today because most of us have been brought up with a different mindset than our "foremothers." We have mostly been brought up in an institutional school setting, apart from our own parents, and were inundated with a focus on having a career, which eventually led to a full-time job outside the home. So, we as modern mothers, choosing to homeschool, have a learning curve to overcome. We must be about allowing the Holy Spirit to "transform" our modern minds into a more relational pattern of family life.

Scriptures for Meditation:
Choose my instruction rather than silver, and **knowledge** rather than pure gold.
–Proverbs 8:10

Therefore, my people are gone into captivity for **lack of knowledge**; and their honorable men are famished, and their multitude are parched with thirst.
–Isaiah 5:13

Prayer for Today: *Thank You, Lord, for the knowledge, wisdom and resources You provide to help me make wise decisions and to understand the history behind homeschooling. Fill me with Your heavenly knowledge as I walk in this modern world. Help me to know what it means to be in the world, but not of the world. Amen.*

Journey of Letting Go

Just as eating against one's will is injurious to health, so studying without a liking for it spoils the memory, and it retains nothing it takes in.
—Leonardo Da Vinci

How often have I forced my children to continue a curriculum that they clearly despised or didn't enjoy simply because 1) I paid a substantial amount of money for it and/or 2) I was absolutely driven by fear that they needed this particular curriculum. How often have I become angry at my child during a math session until they were breaking down in tears, and I was virtually ripping my hair out!

It's not worth it, my friends. Take it from one who knows, one who has struggled with a tendency to control—nearly my entire life as a parent. Once a child is reduced to tears or sullen with stubbornness over a subject or curriculum, it's over. They most likely will retain nothing. The brain circuits literally shut down. They become overloaded and nothing will stick.

As I said, it's a journey. I am finally learning, after approximately 15 years of being a stay-at-home/homeschooling mom, that it's okay to let go. It's not just okay, it's a healthy and freeing choice. It's a good choice! To be led by the fear of others' opinions, the fear of failure, the fear of getting "behind" is not a healthy place to be. It's a burdensome place to be. And this isn't the life the Lord came to give us as homeschool moms. He came to give us abundant joy and peace. But that means we must make a choice to let go and follow His Spirit.

So today, let's remember the words of Da Vinci, genius that he was. Let's try to relax and have more fun with our children. Let's focus on enjoying them for this short time we have them.

Scripture for Meditation:
So Christ has truly set us free. Now make sure that you stay free, and don't get tied up again in slavery to the law. –Galatians 5:1

Prayer for Today: *Lord, help me to walk in freedom today from the bondage of fear. Empower me to come alongside my children and learn with them, to follow their interests and not be worried and anxious if we are not following our curriculum to a "t." May we walk in joy, peace and love with our families and make memories that will be shared for a lifetime. Amen.*

Identity Crisis

Spiritual identity means we are not what we do or what people say about us. And we are not what we have. We are the beloved daughters and sons of God.
—Henri Nouwen

The idea of identity is really important for us to explore, when it comes to our role as "homeschool mom." There have literally been times when I have gazed at myself in the mirror and wondered, *"Who are you?"* There have been times in this journey when I have lost my sense of self. I felt I had lost who I really was as an individual with gifts, talents and dreams.

Educating our children at home can sometimes seem like a daunting and all-consuming task. We can become so immersed in the daily routines, the curriculums, house work, cooking, etc, that we can begin to find our identity and our worth in our "role", instead of in being a daughter of the King. Therefore, when we feel we are doing an "okay" or a "good" job, then we feel like we have worth. Conversely, when things don't look so good, or we get "behind," we begin to feel our identity is slipping, as well as our worth as a person.

This is why it is extremely important for us as moms to find our true and lasting identity in the One who created us for Himself. It is only in that secure place that we can ultimately thrive, where we know we are loved for who we are, not what we do. We cannot rely on our identity as a homeschooler to give us a sense of worth or value. While it may be a "calling" the Lord has brought into our lives, it's not where we find our sense of self. It is in our Savior alone.

Scripture for Meditation: Follow God's example, therefore, as dearly loved children and walk in the way of love, just as Christ loved us and gave himself up for us as a fragrant offering and sacrifice to God.
–Ephesians 5:1-2

Prayer for Today: *Dear Lord, it's so easy to lose our sense of self and to try and find our identity in what we "do" instead of "who" we are. Help us to be aware of our identity in Christ, and remind us of Your love and acceptance of us as Your beloved daughters. In Jesus' Name, Amen.*

Hope Shifting

A Christian will part with anything rather than his hope; he knows that hope will keep the heart both from aching and breaking, from fainting and sinking; he knows that hope is a beam of God, a spark of glory, and that nothing shall extinguish it till the soul be filled with glory.
—Thomas Brooks

Hope.

It's something we all have as believers in Christ. We have the hope of glory—the hope of life eternal spent in the presence of our Creator and Lord. It's something that is promised to us in God's Word, and it gives us great comfort and the ability to persevere through the trials of this life.

But sometimes our hope can become misplaced. It can "shift" to something temporal; something other than Jesus alone. In homeschooling circles, it is easy for us to begin unconsciously putting our hope for our children into the process of home education. We somehow begin to have the idea that if we homeschool, then our children will certainly be saved and have a solid relationship with the Lord. Somehow we begin to misplace our hope in a process or way of life, instead of "The Way and The Life" Himself.

While the choice to home educate can be a tool that the Lord can use in the lives of our children to draw them closer to Him and to help disciple them, it is not where our hope should be found. The Cross of Jesus is the place where all hope is to be found, regardless of educational choices. It took me some years of misplaced hope to come to this realization that my children were sinners, in need of a Savior, regardless of how they are raised. Homeschooling will not change their hearts; only the Holy Spirit can do that. He is the One who draws them into a relationship with Jesus Christ.

So, don't carry this burden of misplaced hopes, my friend. It is a heavy burden that can weigh you down and make the homeschooling journey more about bondage than freedom. Cast all your cares for your children on to the Savior and let Him carry them all. In fact, He already has and will continue to do so. Put your hope firmly in His sacrifice and His Spirit, and trust Him to do the work of bringing your children into a saving knowledge of Jesus.

Scripture for Meditation:
I pray that God, the source of hope, will fill you completely with joy and peace because you trust in him. Then you will overflow with confident hope through the power of the Holy Spirit.
–Romans 15:13

Prayer for Today:
Father, remind me of where to place my true hope. Jesus is my eternal hope. Help me to guide my children daily into the Living Hope they can only find through a relationship with You. I cast all my burdens upon You and ask You to keep my eyes fixed on You. Amen.

Holy Hugs

When you are hugging a child, always be the last one to let go. You never know how long they need it.
—Author Unknown

As I was thinking of another topic to write about, I asked my 11-year old son, "Micah, what do you think moms need to hear about? What should I write to them?" His response was short and sweet. "That they need lots of hugs?" I said "Yes, son, you are so right! We all do, don't we?"

So today I will write about hugs. Hugs are extremely important in my homeschooling day. It's difficult to stay angry and frustrated when a child hugs you or when you start your day with hugs for each of your children. Not only do they benefit, but so do we as moms!

Hugging is emotionally healing and healthy. It warms our souls and creates a stronger bonding and attachment with our children. When on the verge of blowing my top over helping with a math problem, a soothing hug helps to settle things down more quickly.

Our Father is in these hugs, I believe. When we hug one another, it's like He is putting His arms around us and holding us, even if it's just for a moment. It's Him whispering, *"I love you, and I am here in this moment with you."*

So, today's lesson plan is to begin to incorporate hugs as an integral part of each day. Let's be intentional about it. Some of us are more naturally "touchy-feely" than others, but no matter what our temperaments, hugs are good for everyone! So hug your big, lanky teenager and hug your feisty little one, tight. It's healing, healthy and bonding!

Scripture for Meditation:
He tends his flock like a shepherd: He gathers the lambs in his arms and carries them close to his heart; He gently leads those that have young.
–Isaiah 40:11

Prayer for Today:
Heavenly Father, thank You for creating hugs. It was all Your design and Your idea. Thank You that when I hug my children, I am giving them a feeling of Your love. And when my children hug me, I can catch a glimpse of Your Loving Presence in the moments of my day. Help me to always hug my children no matter how old they get and to bond with them in a deep and meaningful way.

Heavenly Tears

Heaven knows we need never be ashamed of our tears, for they are rain upon the blinding dust of earth, overlying our hard hearts. I was better after I had cried, than before—more sorry, more aware of my own ingratitude, more gentle.
—Charles Dickens, *Great Expectations*

In this life, there are tumultuous and rocky times. And in our homeschooling journey, it is no different. There will be tears. Just expect it and know that it's okay. We've all been there...locked in the bathroom, staring in the mirror, trying to hold back the tears and then just letting them flow. Sometimes, we crumple to our knees and just sit there in the floor, wondering who we are, what we are doing, and how we got to this place!

If you have yet to experience these times, just know that *when* you do, *not if,* that you are normal. You will make it. Tears can be a healthy way to let our feelings out, to let them flow. Sometimes, days at home with our children are so trying on our nerves, on our patience, that we just want to run away and hide; we just want to be anywhere but there!

Our Father understands, and He is with us in those very moments when we don't think we can do this anymore, when we don't think we were cut out for this. He is there, and we are never alone with our tears and our pain. Our tears can make us softer, and when our children see our tears, they learn that it's okay to be upset sometimes. They can also learn to show compassion to others.

The Lord uses all the tears of our life for His glory, as we surrender to Him. In ourselves, we can do nothing, but in Him, he takes everything and turns it into something good, even our tears.

Scripture for Meditation:
Those who sow with tears will reap with songs of joy. Those who go out weeping, carrying seed to sow, will return with songs of joy, carrying sheaves with them.
–Psalm 126:5-6

Prayer for Today:
Abba Father, I put my emotions in Your loving hands today. Help me to be secure in Your love even when the tears flow, and I feel confused, hurt, angry or disappointed. I want to sense your presence with me even in those times in my day at home with my children. One day all the tears will be wiped away. Thank You, Lord. Amen.

Hang On

When you come to the end of your rope, tie a knot and hang on.
—Franklin D. Roosevelt

How many times have I been at the "end of my rope" on this homeschooling journey? How many times during the school year do I say to myself, "I can't do this anymore."? Too many times to count, I'm afraid. It seems to be a fairly common thought for many moms.

Yes, my sister, there are many moments that we feel like giving up and throwing in the towel on homeschooling. This could be due to a variety of reasons. Maybe our children are strong-willed, and every day is a battle from sun up to sunset. Or maybe we are obsessive about following our schedules rigidly and flexibility is very difficult for us. Maybe the noise, arguing, and confusion of simply being with your children all day is more than a sane brain can handle.

Whatever the case, most of us have been there. I know I have! I understand the anxiety, the feeling of being overwhelmed and misunderstood, unappreciated and invisible. But it's at this very point that the Lord can speak into our hearts His eternal words of peace and comfort. His Spirit can encourage us to rest in Him, to find our strength and peace in Him alone.

Nothing we ever do for the Lord is in vain. Did you hear that my sweet sister? I will say it again. *Nothing we ever do for the Lord will ever be overlooked by Him.* He rewards faith. He rewards perseverance. And as we press on following His calling and His lead, He will be with us and bless us. The fruit may not be evident for years to come, but I believe it will be there. And we will never regret this journey with our eyes fixed on Jesus.

Scripture for Meditation:
Therefore, my dear brothers and sisters, stand firm. Let nothing move you. Always give yourselves fully to the work of the Lord, because you know that your labor in the Lord is not in vain.
–1 Corinthians 15:58

Prayer for Today: *Father, sometimes I don't think I can bear another day on this homeschooling journey. I feel like this is all a mistake, yet I will walk by faith and cling to what I believe You have called me to do. Help me to walk with You one day at a time, one moment at a time. Amen.*

Grace Upon Grace...For Me!

Sometimes the journey of homeschooling can seem like a burden that is too heavy for us to carry. It may, at times, seem like the Lord has asked us to take on a task that is far beyond what we can handle. And to be honest, it is more than I can handle!

But that's a good thing.

Why? Because as I learn to give up my need to control and fix everything and everyone around me and simply *trust* in my Heavenly Father, He pours out His abundant *grace* to carry me through what only He can do *through* me.

In essence, the very *best* place for us to start on this journey is by admitting that *we can't do this* in our own strength and ability, but by *His grace alone*, we can choose daily to walk by faith, taking one day at a time, and trusting that our Father will carry us, guide us and lead us in this wonderful adventure called homeschooling.

Scripture for Meditation:
For out of His fullness (abundance) we have all received [all had a share and we were all supplied with] one grace after another *and* spiritual blessing upon spiritual blessing *and* even favor upon favor *and* gift [heaped] upon gift.
—John 1:16 (Amplified)

Prayer for Today: *Father, as Your child, You have poured out an abundance of grace, blessing and favor upon my life. Thank You for this, Lord, and help me to remember that it's not up to me to carry the weight of this journey myself, but to cast all upon You, trusting that Your grace is more than enough.*

Godly Imperfection

The imperfections of a man, his frailties, his faults, are just as important as his virtues. You can't separate them. They're wedded.
—Henry Miller

There is an issue being lodged in the hearts and minds of many homeschooling moms these days. I know I have certainly struggled with this deception myself. It is the idea that in order to truly help someone else, we need to "have it all together", ourselves. We somehow think that we must have attained a certain spiritual level before we can truly be effective in reaching out to another mom or family in need.

Where did this idea originate? How did we come to believe such a concept? Well, I think it's partly due to false teachings that circulate within the homeschooling community. We have this idea that somehow every other family has it more together than we do; therefore, how could we possibly be of any use to someone else when we ourselves feel so inadequate? How can we give any advice when we feel at a loss, day to day, in our own homeschooling journey?

Friends, I want to assure you of the truth today—there is no spiritual perfection you must attain before the Lord can use you in His Kingdom. And another truth is this: No one has it all together! There is no homeschooling family that has attained perfection in this life. What qualifies someone to help another? All that is required is a willing, open, compassionate and transparent heart. That's all. *Jesus qualifies the called; He doesn't call the qualified.*

Remember this today. You, dear Mama, have so much to offer to your fellow moms. We need each other. We need each other to be real and transparent in our struggles, to share all of life's joys, as well as the valleys. The Lord can, and will, use you to help others. Just be open and ready to see His Spirit at work in you.

Scripture for Meditation:

Is there any encouragement from belonging to Christ? Any comfort from his love? Any fellowship together in the Spirit? Are your hearts tender and compassionate? Then make me truly happy by agreeing wholeheartedly with each other, loving one another, and working together with one mind and purpose. Don't be selfish; don't try to impress others. Be humble, thinking of others as better than yourselves.

–Philippians 2:1-3

Prayer for Today:

I am all too aware of my imperfections, weaknesses, struggles and frailties today, Lord. Yet, in spite of all those, I desire for You to use me in Your Kingdom to encourage other moms in their homeschool journey. Please help me to show compassion and a transparent heart and to reach out to others who need help. Amen.

From Doldrums to Delight

Every morning when the sunlight opens our eyes, our first though should be, "I'm a child of the Father! I've been chosen by Him to be a member of His family! His peace, His joy, and His love are my legacy, my inheritance - and I can draw upon His riches every moment of every day, no matter what my circumstances may be.
—Ray Stedman (Our Riches in Christ)

Oh, to wake up with this thought each morning! How wonderful it would be! Unfortunately, far too often I wake up with a very opposite view of my day. I'm already dreading the day before I ever get out of bed! I don't even want to leave my room because of the weariness and routine of another day.

Yes, homeschooling can be hard. Days can be long and difficult. Arguments, bickering, complaining and whining can bring even the most optimistic outlook down to the pits. Dealing with our own flesh and that of our children on a moment by moment basis can be enough to send anyone to the funny farm!

Yet, as children of God, we have been given everything! We truly have it all. Our part is simply to acknowledge this and *believe* the Truth. As our minds dwell on this truth, our outlook begins to change, and we begin to see with eternal perspective. This is the perspective we need to persevere and not grow weary in our homeschool journey. Knowing we are His beloved children, dearly loved by Him, can transform our days from the doldrums to a delight!

Scripture for Meditation: Ephesians 1:17-22

Prayer for Today: *Thank You, Abba Father, that I am Your beloved child. Help me to start each day in the realization and acknowledgement of this great truth. I pray that as I believe this more and more that this Truth will transform my homeschooling journey from glory to glory. Amen!*

Forgiveness Sets Us Free

To forgive is to set a prisoner free and discover that the prisoner was you.
—Philip Yancey

The homeschooling journey affords us abundant opportunities to both give and receive forgiveness. While the sheer amount of time we spend with our children is one of the great benefits of homeschooling, it also comes with a great price—the price of seeing the *"not-so-lovely"* sides of ourselves, which we would often rather not see.

The ugliness and selfishness of our flesh can be starkly real, especially at times when we are tired, weary, ill, or when our children are defiant, whining, hateful and foolish. It is very easy to begin to condemn ourselves for our mistakes in parenting and homeschooling. We struggle to forgive ourselves when we fail to live and be the examples we want our children to follow.

Yet, we must learn to be gentle with ourselves and to forgive ourselves for our mistakes and failures. After all, our Father forgives us. He is merciful when we cry out to Him. In Him, we are washed clean. Therefore, we must accept this forgiveness and love daily in order to be able to give it to others, namely our children and spouses. When we forgive ourselves, we are free to experience the grace, love and goodness of our God in a new and refreshing way.

Scripture for Meditation:
For You, Lord, *are* good, and ready to forgive, and abundant in mercy to all those who call upon You.
–Psalm 86:5

Prayer for Today: *Abba, thank You for Your willingness and goodness to forgive my many mistakes. Give me the grace to forgive myself and to release myself into the great love and freedom that You provide through your Son. Amen.*

First Things First

We can get too easily bogged down in the academic part of homeschooling, a relatively minor part of the whole, which is to raise competent, caring, literate, happy people.
—Diane Flynn Keith

What is our mission as homeschool moms? What are we trying to accomplish by keeping our children at home with us each day, instead of sending them off to an institutional school? What is the focus of all that we do each day?

While we probably all agree with the quote above, it's much harder to actually live that out. At least it is for me! It's one thing for me to say it and quite another to actually put it into action. Yet, the truth is that while academics are important, the relationship and bonds that we are making with our children is what will stand the true test of time. And the more I remember this, and put it in the forefront of my mind, the more joyful my children and I will likely be.

How do we raise "competent, caring, literate, happy people?" Will it just automatically happen as a byproduct of our choice to keep and teach our children in the home? I don't believe so. It takes an effort, a focus, a decision that this pursuit will be our main goal and our main purpose in schooling at home. The connection with our children and their hearts will be priority number one over and above all else. With the pursuit of a loving relationship with our children at the forefront of our minds, I believe the Lord blesses all the rest!

Scripture for Meditation:
So now I am giving you a new commandment: Love each other. Just as I have loved you, you should love each other. Your love for one another will prove to the world that you are my disciples."
–John 13:34-35

Prayer for Today: *Heavenly Father, I know that relationships are what are first and foremost important in this life. You gave your Son, Jesus, so You could have a relationship with us. Help me to put the relationships with my children and their wellbeing first over their academic knowledge. I pray for the grace to lay down any fears and anxiety that prevent me from making this my first goal in home schooling. Amen.*

Crucial Friendships

One of the most beautiful qualities of true friendship is to understand and to be understood.
—Lucius Annaeus Seneca

The journey of homeschooling can initially be a very lonely undertaking. As moms and dads, we have chosen to step outside of the "normal and/or acceptable" approach in the education of our children. We are on the "fringe" in many ways, and that can be an isolating place. Seeking out the fellowship of other like-minded moms and families becomes of utmost importance to help secure the longevity of this endeavor.

We were never meant to be an island unto ourselves in homeschooling, or any other facet of life for that matter. When I started on this journey, I had the attitude that I could do this all on my own. Of course, I relied on the Lord, but I had the attitude that it was He and I. I wasn't aware of just how vital it would be to have the support of others who were on this same journey. I went through some very dark and depressing times, until I realized that I simply *could not* do this on my own, that I needed support and the help of other mom friends.

As moms, we may also have a tendency to *overly* rely upon our husbands to give us all the support and encouragement we need in our homeschooling adventure. As a general rule, and in my own personal experience, husbands cannot give us all the support we need. They weren't created to be our "all-in-all." They can be wonderful sources of strength, and it is crucial that we have their support and blessing. Yet, we need to surround ourselves with those who understand us first-hand and all that we are experiencing.

Scripture for Meditation:
An honest answer is like a kiss of friendship.
–Proverbs 24:26

Prayer for Today: *Father in heaven, guide me and lead me by Your Spirit to the friends You want in my life. Help me to surround myself with moms who are supportive and encouraging, and help me to be a support to others on the homeschooling journey. Give me the grace to realize that I cannot do this alone, that I need friends to walk with me. Amen.*

Controlling Anger

Be not angry that you cannot make others as you wish them to be, since you cannot make yourself as you wish to be.
—Thomas a Kempis

The issue of anger…it may be many a homeschool mom's best-kept secret! I know I have certainly struggled with this issue during my years of educating my children at home. Even approaching this subject can often bring great shame and self-condemnation on moms who tend toward having "short fuse" with their offspring.

I often think that the anger stems from a desire to *control*; a desire to change our children into something or someone we wish they would be. We often have very lofty and idealistic goals for our children. Sometimes these goals are even unattainable and border on perfection. No wonder we stay angry and frustrated when we have set unattainable goals for ourselves and those in our home!

It's not that we should have zero expectations of our children, there are healthy and godly goals and visions that we have as children of our Father. He has created us to know Him and love Him above all things. And we are called to trust Him to mold, change and transform our children's lives from the inside out. We can never force this to happen.

I certainly still deal with anger. It is a weakness that I must surrender daily to my loving Father who is compassionate and understanding. But being transparent and open about my struggles helps us to overcome them. And through these trials, we can help others in their weakness and bring comfort, hope and healing.

Scripture for Meditation:
My dear brothers and sisters, take note of this: Everyone should be quick to listen, slow to speak and slow to become angry, because human anger does not produce the righteousness that God desires.
–James 1:19-20

Prayer for Today: *Dear Father, I come to You and surrender all control into Your loving hands today. Help me to accept the things I cannot change, to change the things I can, and give me the wisdom to know the difference. Amen.*

By His Spirit

God, grant me the serenity to accept the things
I cannot change;
The courage to change the things I can;
And the wisdom to know the difference.
—Serenity Prayer

While many people only associate this prayer with the ministry of Alcoholics Anonymous, this famous prayer can apply to a variety of situations and circumstances in our lives, including our homeschooling. Have you ever tried to change your child's personality? Have you ever tried to change someone else in your home, to no avail? Chances are, if you are anything like me, the answer is a definite yes. But chances are, also like me, that it proved to be a royal failure!

Why is this and how does this affect us in regards to educating our children? The truth is, no matter how much we may try to force, manipulate or implement a change in our child's attitude or personality, we cannot change them. We do not have that power. It is utterly outside of our own human abilities.

Often we hear that the only person we can change is ourselves. While there is truth in that statement, it is also true that we *can't* change ourselves. It takes the power of the Holy Spirit to do that in our lives. It's not our own strength that can affect change, but our reliance on the Perfect One whom has already given us all things by His blood and sacrifice. It is our faith in the finished work of Jesus and abiding in Him that effects the greatest change in our lives.

So, can we trust Jesus to affect change in our children in the same way He affects change in us? Can we let go of our need for control and let Him have his way in them? This takes wisdom; knowing when to intervene and guide and when to let go and watch Him work. Therefore, we pray for wisdom, and in the meantime, in the waiting, we pray for serenity, for peace that passes all understanding. It's a life long journey, my friends. But it's worth it.

Scripture for Meditation:
Then he said to me, "This is what the Lord says to Zerubbabel: It is not by force nor by strength, but by my Spirit, says the Lord of Heaven's Armies.
–Zechariah 4:6

Prayer for Today:
Jesus, I ask You for heavenly wisdom today for my children and homeschooling. I pray You would show me what I can change and what I can't, what I am to be involved with and when to wait upon you today. Help me to accept my children as they are, and in the areas where they are weak, to pray for them and wait upon Your perfect timing in their lives. Amen.

All About Attitude

Nothing can stop the man with the right mental attitude from achieving his goal; nothing on earth can help the man with the wrong mental attitude.
—Thomas Jefferson

According to Merriam-Webster, attitude is defined *as "the way you think and feel about someone or something: a feeling or way of thinking that affects a person's behavior."* An obvious and wise question we need to ask ourselves as homeschooling moms in light of this quote by Jefferson is "How is our mental attitude towards the education of our children, and of our children themselves?"

It may seem obvious to us that we should have a very positive attitude towards homeschooling and towards our children, yet often, we don't—at least I don't, and I don't think I am alone in this! It's so easy to become negative in our attitudes toward the "daily grind" of our homeschooling days. We sometimes fall into the mantra of "same old, same old," when someone asks us how our days went. Or we name off a list of complaints about how we never seem to get "anything done" or we constantly feel "behind," etc. I am guilty mom number 1 when it comes to this!

Yet, if what Jefferson wrote is correct, and I happen to believe it is, then how must I change this about myself? I believe there is biblical support for the concept that our thoughts affect our actions. What we dwell on daily will certainly set the course for our homeschooling adventures. So what do we dwell on? What *should* we dwell on?

What personally helps me "refocus" is to begin to dwell on how blessed I am to be able to have the freedom to homeschool. It is a privilege that I have. When my mind wanders into feeling like educating my children is a burden, then I must redirect my thoughts to the *truth*. The truth is my children are a blessing not a burden, and it is a privilege to be able to "do life" together through this homeschooling journey, for better or worse.

Scripture for Meditation:
And now, dear brothers and sisters, one final thing. Fix your thoughts on what **is** true, and honorable, and right, and pure, and lovely, and admirable. Think about things that are excellent and worthy of praise.
–Philippians 4:8

Prayer for Today: *Dear Abba, empower me today to turn my thoughts toward a positive direction. Help me to focus on what a blessing and privilege it is to be able to be home with my children, doing life together. May my attitude reflect Your character and Your love in my home, and may Your grace encourage me when I make mistakes throughout my day. May Your Spirit take my mind captive for Jesus. Amen.*

A Burden Beyond Compare

Comparison is the death of joy.
—Mark Twain

As women, we often fall into the trap of comparing ourselves to other women, of comparing our husbands to other men, of comparing our children, our homes, our lives, the list is endless of the ways we can compare ourselves. When we choose the journey of home education, this is just another area where we are lured into the trap of comparison in an even more insidious way.

Once we begin homeschooling, we compare our curriculums, our educational philosophy, our domestic abilities, our teaching ability, the cleanliness of our homes, how our children behave, and on and on the list goes. This comparison brings with it a yoke; a burden that is extremely heavy to carry. And often we don't even realize we are carrying this unnecessary load upon our backs. It weighs us down. It silently steals our joy. And one day we get up, and we have lost the passion we once had for our choice to educate our children at home.

How do we combat this tendency toward comparison? How do we begin to be set free from its tenacious grasp? Well, first, there are no formulas. There is no 3-step program to help us overcome this. Bummer! Wouldn't it be nice if that were the case? I think the first place to start is to acknowledge this tendency and to name it for what it is...a burden we were never meant to carry. The Lord never intended for us to live in this place of endless comparison. He desires to lead our families in a very individual and unique way. Our Father didn't create robots. He doesn't want us all to look the same! He loves diversity!

So, today, let's take the first glimpse in realizing that we can lay that comparison burden down at Jesus' feet. We can find rest and reassurance and unconditional love there. Whatever curriculum we choose to glorify Him, whatever teaching style He leads us to use according to our unique children and our own particular personalities, whatever it all my look like, it's okay. It's not only okay, it's good and great! Believe that.

Scripture for Meditation:
Then Jesus said, "Come to me, all of you who are weary and carry heavy burdens, and I will give you rest. Take my yoke upon you. Let me teach you, because I am humble and gentle at heart, and you will find rest for your souls. For my yoke is easy to bear, and the burden I give you is light."
–Matthew 11:28-30

Prayer for Today: *Abba Father, I acknowledge my tendency to compare myself with other homeschooling moms and families. I ask for your grace to help me overcome this and to see others and myself as unique individuals each on our unique paths of life. Empower me to celebrate the differences we have instead of feeling anxious or fearful that I should be someone different that I am. In Jesus Name, Amen.*

Who I Am

When I discover who I am, I'll be free.
—Ralph Ellison, *Invisible Man*

Who we are...
Our identity...

Over the years last 16 years of being a stay-at-home, homeschooling mom, I must say that I have struggled with this concept on a continual basis, to varying degrees. When my children were babies and toddlers, it seemed both logical and practical to me to stay at home and raise them myself. It also seemed like the best choice from the many books and articles that I read. As the children have grown older, the black and whites of yesteryear have given way to subtle forms of gray. I have often looked in the mirror and wondered, *"Who are you? What has happened to you? Who is the real you?"*

I can honestly say that I have not arrived at an answer that totally satisfies me. I still wrestle within myself about this issue. Yet, I do believe the Lord is continually speaking to my heart that my truest and freest identity is who I am in Him. This is the core of my being. This is the most important "who" that I am. And this is where my eternal value and worth lies.

I've often been envious of others who have a "career" with an official title. People ask my husband what he does for a living, and he says, "I'm an engineer." I always feel very proud of him because of this. And then, I think of myself and wonder how he could be proud of me as his wife without a title other than "mom" and "wife." Oh, I know these are hideous lies of the enemy of our souls, yet the thoughts do occur.

So, I guess my encouragement for us is simply that, regardless of our careers, titles or lack of both, our true identity is that we are children of the Most High King. If we have made Jesus our personal Messiah and Lord, then He is indeed our identity in the purest and most important sense of the word. And nothing and no one can take that away from us.

Scripture for Meditation:
I have been crucified with Christ; and it is no longer I who live, but Christ lives in me, and the life which I now live in the flesh I live by faith in the Son of God, who loved me and gave Himself up for me.
–Galatians 2:20

Prayer for Today:
Father, thank You that You have made me your child through Your Son Jesus Christ. I have come into Your family and have been bought with a price. I am fearfully and wonderfully made by You. Help me to believe this in the deepest part of my being. Infuse this truth upon my heart and mind so that I can walk, live and breathe in this reality on a daily basis. Amen.

ABOUT THE AUTHOR

Tina Nahid has been a busy stay-at-home, homeschooling mom and wife and has 3 children. She is very active within her local homeschool support group and desires to encourage other moms on their journey. She has a M.A. in English and has had devotions published in a variety of publications over the years. Tina enjoys reading, writing, date nights with her hubby, traveling, mom's night out, exercising, mission trips and field trips with her kids.

45287590R00037

Made in the USA
San Bernardino, CA
04 February 2017